Best Man Wedding Speeches

How to Deliver Best Man Great Wedding Speeches with Examples of Funny and Memorable Touch

By
Luna Pearl

First Printing, 2012

Printed in the United States of America

Terms of Use

You are given a non-transferable, "personal use" license to this book. You cannot distribute it or share it with other individuals.

Also, there are no resale rights or private label rights granted when purchasing this book. In other words, it is for your own personal use only.

Best Man Wedding Speeches

How to Deliver Best Man Great Wedding Speeches with Examples of Funny and Memorable Touch

Table of Contents

Getting Started 9

Heartfelt and Memorable Wedding Toast for the Best Man 13

Fire up Your Self Esteem! It's Your Buddy's Greatest Day 17

Speak from Your Heart with the Touch of Proper Humors 25

The Structure of Your Speech 31

Preparations for Your Speech 37

Great Ideas of a Best Man Toast................................... 41

Things to Do and Not to Do.. 45

Elements to Consider before Writing the Speech......... 49

Posture and Etiquettes for the Best Man 51

Best Man Basic Speech Format..................................... 55

Personalize Your Speech 59

Watch Out of the 'Slip of Tongue'................................ 63

Facts You Can't Go Without 69

A Formal Speech Example... 71

Wedding Jokes and Quotes... 73

Best Man's Different Roles.. 83

Structural Steps to Write a Hilarious and Heartfelt Speech 87

End of the Line.. **89**

Getting Started

Great wedding speeches typically are carefully thought out and organized well in advance of the wedding reception. A good speech will touch all the high points that you wish to deliver. There are specific elements to consider when writing these types of speeches, and all can come together to help you deliver a message that hits just the right tone for the celebration.

As with any speech, you are going to want to organize your thoughts for presenting to the reception attendees. You can start with an outline so that you remember to cover everything you wish to say to the newlyweds. Keep in mind that this may be an once-in-a-lifetime event for you, so it is best to make every word count.

Consider any memories you may wish to mention about the couple during your delivery. Remember to keep your audience in mind with these stories. A humorous but engaging story can work great to help set the tone for the rest of the speech and be something that the bride and groom can enjoy.

Stories from childhood can be the best to make as a focal point in your presentation. Not only can these anecdotes show the contrast of the people you are making a toast to today, but it also may touch on something that is reflective of them now. The story also could tug at heartstrings if your anecdote revolves around something sentimental.

Wedding speeches can work if you give yourself ample time to organize and collect your thoughts on paper. If you keep your goals in mind on what you want to say and how to say it, the entire speech can be easier. Many members of the wedding party may remember your well-delivered speech for years to come.

The Best Man's Role

Weddings are one of the most important events in a person's life. It is a day that marks a union of two souls into one, where the couple takes vows and binds their love for each other. The wedding day is magical and special, ad the feeling that the couple to be married go through, is completely out of the world. Preparation for this day begins weeks and months prior to the big day.

Both the bride and groom's special friends are mostly appointed to fulfill each and every responsibilities and preparations. Like the bride has her bride's maids and maid of honor to support, and help her through it all, the groom has groom's men and his Best Man. They are the ones who take all the responsibilities. There is no doubt that being a Best Man is usually the groom's best friend.

However, in some cases he can also be the person who is close to him. He plays a very vital role for making the wedding a success.

He is like an anchor, who keeps the sailing ship in place, like the captain of a ship, directing and maintaining schedules and plans. He is like glue that sticks until the end. The Best Man is given the responsibility of making the wedding speech. So, he must put in a lot of effort to make the best speech for the success and get applauded too. This is no normal or regular speech; it has to be an Oscar winning speech. All eyes would be glued to you and your speech would make the groom look good, so you cannot afford to lose on that, at least!

A wedding speech goes along with the toast to the newly weds. The speech does not mean a lecture, so stick to short and meaningful one. Take maximum of 2 minutes and not more than that because people are more eager to see the first dance of the newly weds, eat the cake and enjoy the champagne. You do not want to bore them with your long speech, and lectures are not meant for the occasion.

The speech of the best man is an important part of any wedding ceremony, and is remembered for years after the special day is over. The speech traditionally is meant to honor the groom but you should not forget the bride and congratulate them together. As a best man, you have been given the position of distinction of honor and responsibility. These speeches are also known as toasts and you should make efforts to prepare them in advance.
Write and prepare your toast prior to the wedding day and if you are a bit introvert, then plan and practice it day and night. Here are some tips and basics of a Best Man speech that you can apply. This would definitely help you

to get a standing ovation from the wedded couple but also from the other guests. Maybe you can get lucky and find your 'to be life partner' here.

Heartfelt and Memorable Wedding Toast for the Best Man

Becoming a Best Man is like becoming a royal guard to the Queen Mother. It is a matter of great pride and honor. Best Man means that you have to be the 'best', and deliver the best speech. It is in fact a moment of sentiment, as you have to stand up and address a toast to the bride and groom, amongst 100's of guests. There is definite pressure as all attention is on you, during those 2 minutes of your speech. You cannot afford to mess it up all, it might sound tough but it is not. Writing a great and meaningful toast is all about creativity and simplicity.

You have to be a bit patient and a little hardworking. This is because the groom has chosen you to be his Best Man after a lot of thinking and discerning; he must have something good about you in his mind. So, you cannot be reluctant and just deliver some hand written speech. Have the faith and give a speech, whereby every word is simply wishing luck, and love to the newly weds!

So, what you have to do first while preparing the speech?

To begin with, you should jot down all your thoughts about the to-be wedded couple quite freely, relating your relationship with them, especially with the groom. Write these questions and try to answer them first:

- How are they known to you?
- Why were you chosen to be the Best Man?

- In describing individual bride and groom, what are the first few adjectives that streams into your mind?
- Groom's state prior to the meeting of his bride and how much has he changed after meeting her.
- How did they meet each other?
- How did the groom tell you about the bride?
- If you happen to be a married person, then how would you give some marriage tips and advice to the couple?
- Can you relate to any special event or anecdotes to illustrate either the groom or the bride?
- Go through sample wedding toasts and jot down few simple ones, just in case that is!

After writing and answering all, you have to utilize them into some entertaining yet heartfelt toasts.

The Beginning: First, you have to begin by giving a brief introduction about yourself, since not all present in the room would know you. It is suggested to excuse you and ask for their attention. Then, introduce yourself and tell about your relationship with the groom. If you want the attention of the guests, it would great if you crack a joke or something or even quote something funny related to marriage. Prior to the speech's end don't forget to give thanks to the host, parents traditionally that of the bride's and if the couple is paying themselves for everything in the wedding, then just say that "we are all delighted" or something "to be present in this beautiful occasion".

The mid: in this stage, all the above notes that you had written would be applicable. It would be good if you tell something funny, or a hilarious story related to the couple, or either of them. However, this should not be anything humiliating, and you should keep that in mind. Talk about your opinion of love, marriage, union etc. tell story or even talk about the changes that has occurred via their relationship. Since, you are the Best Man; you ought be close and know the groom much better but always maintain a balanced toast and speak about both the bride and the groom.

Avoid long speeches, as others will not be interested in your ramble. One major no-no in a speech is, talking about ex-girlfriends or relationships. You should simply avoid it along with adult content, since the guests would be inclusive of elderly people and children. Lastly, remember that sincerity always takes you a long way, so if you speak from the heart and be honest about everything, then nothing would be wrong!

Closing of the speech: It is advisable to end your toast or the Best Man speech with a traditional toast, wish or also a blessing for the couple. Raise the glass of champagne or wine with congratulations; salute or cheers resounding and then remember to take a sip of the toast.

It would be better if you write the toast on a note, card or paper etc. and then practice for sometime. Try to avoid reading directly from the paper or note. You can also ask some other friend present in the room to provide you with some feedback. After this, you can relax and enjoy the rest of the evening.

Toast delivering tips: In spite of being nerve racked and jittery, do not forget to deliver your speech clearly and loudly. It will be easy because there would be a microphone, hopefully. You have to do some enunciation.

Believe it or not, it is completely worse case and useless to hear a few minutes of continuous rambling!

Drinking a lot prior to your speech is bad. You might take a drink for loosening up or something but avoid drinking like a fish. You would only make a mockery of yourself and nothing.

Avoid reading from the card directly since the words are meant to be heartfelt not by heart! Paraphrase the words and lines that you have written and maintain a sentiment. You can have the notes as prompters but do not forget to lose eye contact with the present people, to whom you are talking. If you happen to lose the paper or note or you get too nervous, then simply give your congratulations to the newly weds or even a cheer but do not go blank!

You must have been told to stand straight and never slouch. Well, it is also necessary during the deliverance of your speech.

Fire up Your Self Esteem! It's Your Buddy's Greatest Day

It has been noticed by all the professional wedding experts that a Best Man is the most potential and important flashpoint of all discontent in a wedding. In fact, ill chosen sentences, drunken humor, etc. made by a best man, can actually ruin the joy and tranquility of a beautiful wedding day! And all this at the cost of thousands and thousands of dollars spend for the wedding's success.

There are common cases, where the damage occurs prior to the knowledge of others about it. He speaks and tells a joke that is completely unacceptable anywhere around. Moreover, after it has been spat out, it becomes too late for anyone present, from the newly weds to their parents to do anything but bear it all with a smile.

At times, a best man is completely clueless regarding is foot in the mouth speech or his blunder. He also has a misconception that he is the party's soul and life, but least does he knows that he is nothing but a party pooper! The reason for all this tolerance is the fact that guests and hosts wants the day to be perfect for both the bride and the groom. They do not want to create a scene; therefore, they try to mellow situations like this and laugh off all the rude and crude remarks that the Best Man makes. So, it follows on and people laugh at whatever he utters and this he mistakes as an encouragement. Being nervous and uncertain, he by mistake assumes that everything he is uttering is being liked and acceptable by all. In fact, all are enjoying his speech, so it is then that he becomes un-stoppable. So, whose fault is it actually?

Partly, the reason is that not all are extroverts, and some even are incapable of standing in front of a crowd or au-dience, leave alone deliver a speech. It is a fact that many best men have made their first public announcement or speech, of their lives. Therefore, most of them even be-come speechless and nervous. They get stage fright at the thought of delivering a speech! As a result, they lose all control and blabber things uncontrollably, taking form into jokes. Later they really regret talking and behaving like that.

There are some best men, who have the least inkling what is needed to say in a speech, right from the beginning un-til the end. These are the ones who fail in their job as a

Best Man. And there are others who have the genuine belief and thought that they have to deliver a speech fit for their pubs' experience and expectations more than the newly weds.

It is therefore advised that every best man having such problem must get professional advice. This way he would be able to draft his speech well and be able to deliver it with aptness and perfection. Enough money is spent on everything for a successful wedding, from the venue to the cake, and then why not spends some extra for expert help.

Using Positive Self-Talk to Fire You Up

Therefore, you are the lucky person, who has been chosen as the Best Man! It is in fact, a great feeling of joy and happiness, to be worthy enough for being a part of someone's most special day. The moment of giving the speech can be full of terror and nervousness. Soon, it dawns, that you have to face a room full of people and deliver some words, which are the pivotal point of a wedding!

It is always better to remember that it is not only you who is getting nervous about making a speech. It is in fact easy for someone to camouflage his or her nerves unlike other best men. So, it is quite natural to have jitters and be nervous about delivering your speech without any blunders.

You should use positive self-talk throughout the day in order to establish a new thinking pattern, you will probably have established a pattern of negative thinking for many years and this will take time to overcome, to start with you should aim to repeat positive self-talk around 50 times throughout the day, this can be achieved by repeating positive statements quietly to yourself or out aloud.

Positive self-talk can be used for many different aspects in your life, it can help you to overcome difficult situations, gain more confidence in yourself, help you to quit habits, recover quicker from illness or make changes to your life in general. Popular phrases or sentences that can be used in positive self-talk include.

- I have an interesting challenge facing me – this could be used when a problem occurs in life or there is some difficulty, rather than looking at the situation in a negative way and thinking I have a problem, thinking of it as a challenge is a much more positive way of dealing with it.

- I like the person I am – this could be used to bolster self-confidence and gain respect about yourself and the person you are, similar statements could be "I am the best", "I am a good person" or "I have many excellent qualities".

- I know I can do this – this could be used if you are faced with a certain task that you would previously doubt yourself capable of conquering, similarly you could say "I have the ability to conquer this" or "this doesn't pose a problem for me"

- I am full of health, energy and vitality – this can be used to encourage good feelings about your health either after you have been sick or while recovering from an illness.

- I am fulfilled as a person – this can be used to encourage good general positive thoughts about yourself and the world in which you live.

Just apply these tips given below and see how you can control your nerve:

- Always think ahead and do the preparation quite in advance. Some are usually urged to do the preparation until the last minute. Writing all the ideas and lines would really warm up you mind prior to the speech making.

- Write the speech in bold and big letters but it does not mean that all of them need to be written in only caps. Just write the important lines, so that they are highlighted and it would become easy for your concentration.

- Do not leave things to chance. If your opening speech has a line like ladies and gentlemen, then do notleave that out, write it. Avoid making assumptions with your opening line and keep it simple. If you need reassurance then you can look into the page and remember that all the words are right in front of your eyes.

- Eating is another way to lower your nerves and professionals advise it too. You get energy from food and it is very vital for nerve control.

- Smile is the best expression that lightens up the environment. So, when you stand up to deliver your speech, remember to smile. This will aid to achieve the exact tone for the speech. And when you witness return of smiles then all your nerves would mellow down.

These are few of the tips that would definitely help in transforming a nervous best man into a confident one and aid him to deliver the best speech ever. If you have paid and spend tones of dollars then why leave the most important duty of speech making on an inexperienced speechmaker. It is tough to give a speech but asking a best man to write it is tough enough. So, it is recommended that professional writer should be asked to write it and make it as personalize as possible.

Speak from Your Heart with the Touch of Proper Humors

Not everyone is outspoken and courageous. If you are the shy one and have been invited to give the best man speech, then you would be pondered with the thought of how you will manage it all. Nevertheless, it is not at all a daunting task. If you prepare and do some homework prior to the wedding day, then it will be just a piece of 'wedding cake'! Some help would definitely make the task easy for you. Remember all the given points, and sway away with your speech.

You are chosen by the groom to represent his biggest day and the reason for you as his choice can be your personality. So, while speaking, do live up to it. It is therefore very important to be yourself all the while. Give explanation in your speech in reference with your relation with the couple, and do not forget to thank the groom for choosing you as his best man, and giving you this honor. Keep your speech general, but include some references of the couple and their families. Limit the duration of the speech, and do not go over board with it. It is a wedding not an election, so guests look forward to enjoy the entire proceedings rather than hear your long speech.

Be loud and clear at the same time. You might be provided with a microphone, so avoid speaking very loudly on it. This would certainly prevent the glasses in the room to break! In your speech, avoid talking about the following: ex-wives, ex-girlfriends and ex-relations of the groom. If you do, then the entire evening would become flushed. Remember, you are not there to humiliate either of the couple, unless you plan to that is! It would be a real bad idea to get a drink before the speech deliverances.

Always remember to thank the bride's parents and her, in making the marriage a success. Then comprehend the people present at last and speak as per the requirement. You can tell a funny incident and how perfect and made for each other are the couple. Please avoid any kind of exaggeration.

Humorous Remarks of the Best Man

You do not have to be all boring and serious, while giving your speech as the best man. It so happens that a hilarious speech draws a lot of attention of all guests. These speeches having humor are ones that are most creative and quite entertaining for the audiences.

However, you have to talk about the bride and groom, while being funny. This is all about confidence, personality and determined learning. The best man must have all these components in his speech, and at the same time be sincere at his responsibility. Your lines should be exact and have all the funny and wit in it. Through this humorous speech, you can actually keep the event alive, if at all it becomes monotonous. There are various websites that provide with the best samples of hilarious speeches made by best men. Some memorable event can become hilarious, related to the life of either the couple. This can be shared in your speech. Just remember not to make it a mockery, which can turn out to be insulting.

Funny Speeches and One Liner

Speeches made by best men are amongst lighter moments in the wedding reception or the rehearsal dinner. It is quite common for best man to make use of with and humor while giving his speech. The reason for such deliverance of such funny ones is that a man and that make this speech too for another man! And it is a universal truth that a man is not that comfortable while talking about emotions and feelings, especially when done on a serious note.

The reflection of the speech made by a best man is on the groom. And it is very much obvious that a best man is a person whom a groom cares and has a great deal of concern. Therefore, it is for this reason that he chose that particular person to be his best man because he suited the role to stand by him all through wedding, the best. People have expectations, as if the best man would deliver a funny speech and joke about his friend – the groom! It is a common trend for a best man to tell some real funny story, related to the groom and perform some mischievous activity or something. But at this point, it is very important to maintain care be cautious not to bring the groom to bad light and that even in front of his newly wedded wife, his family and the rest of his guests.

You can be really funny and mention how flirtatious the groom was, but spilling the beans and relating too much to funny incidents about his ex relationships can be hazardous. This would only mean that your speech is not funny anymore. Discretion is needed and you should draw a line from being funny to insulting! When delivering funny speeches, a best man's focus should be more on the groom than the prospective maid of honor! You should stick to his qualities both as a friend and as a person. Outline and jot down what you believe in and talk about his best qualities in being a great future husband. You can joke and poke fun at him on becoming a terrible husband but the examples that you would cite out should be safe. They should not highlight what is not attractive, and bad in habits. Avoid anything that the groom or the bride's parents would be against or would not approve of, after all it is a new beginning for the groom, so you have no rights to jeopardize it!

Remember to keep it simple and light. All you are trying is to appeal and grab the attention of a room full of people. This room has people of all ages, so one joke might be hilarious for the groom's brother but it would be outrageous for his mother. So, be careful and mind all your jokes, save it all for the bachelor party. Try not to hurt the sentiments of all present, especially of the bride and groom.

One-liners: A best man speech one line should be 'classy', as it a day of importance for both the bride and groom. Speech made by their best man is what a couple would remember for the rest of their lives, whenever they are flipping through the picture album or watching their video tape. Therefore, messing up a speech or mangling it would mean marking it in the pages of embarrassing moments in the history. So, it always better to get it correct in the first instances itself.

One liners used by a best man can either make or break the speech. So, the decision is your, whether you want to end up as a standup comedian or known for delivering a hearty toast for the couple. You would come across many sources and websites that mislead the users, citing that a speech made by a best man is more like an open mice affair at a forum or so. Well, the reality is that it is not. It is rather one of the most highlighted days of a newly wedded couple's life.

Humor in a speech does relief stress and adds a good laugh amongst all. If you go overboard with the entire humor concept then it would become a bad thing. It is a part of the deal that a best man throws some goof ups related to the groom, with one-liners and anecdotes, as long as all is in good shape. Make use of one-liner and jokes that are natural and light at the same time. Be sure that the humor is stuck with the people present.

While using one-liner via a speech, let it be connected to the groom or the bride. Else, they would be bad jokes, instead of hilarious. Use these jokes on the basis of a story; about elements like first dates, couples or also funny things that had taken place during the wedding preparations etc. Corny and really old-fashionedone-liner would put off the wedding party to sleep or it would be completely unacceptable. Do not let the people be predictable about your one-liner. Use them with an air, class and an attitude. Corniest of corniest ones would be sounding funny and acceptable.

The Structure of Your Speech

Preparation is key in wedding speeches. Practicing delivery, tone and style can help you to avoid embarrassing glitches in front of others. If you take the preparation in small stages, you can create a successful presentation filled with remarks appreciated by the bride and groom. Every word in this type of celebratory presentation should resonate with exactly the right message to attendees at the reception. You can begin by making an outline so that you do not leave out any details worth mentioning. This also can help you sharpen delivery overall and keep the speech concise.

If you are at a loss for capturing the moment in your own words, you can peruse books and sources online for famous quotes that may help you capture your thoughts perfectly. There may be just the right one that describes the couple in familiar terms to the audience. You can search by speaker or topic to help you find the right quote. Remember to keep all remarks positive so that the tone remains uplifting.

You may want to include special memories looking back on the bride or groom. With all things shared that may be private, remember to keep the tone simple, straightforward and appropriate for all in attendance. Fun stories can help personalize the rest of your delivery as you move toward more formal remarks wishing them an enjoyable life together.

The memories that you offer in your speech may extend to the bride and groom's childhood, if appropriate for the rest of your delivery. Think about whether there is a story from their youth that might work well for retelling on their wedding day for others to enjoy. As always, make sure it is appropriate for all who may be listening and all ages of your audience.

Before the big day, you may want to pick someone to listen to your speech in private to share comments and analyze your method of delivery. This type of review may be a good opportunity also to see whether you should add or remove anything in the speech. What may sound good to you might receive a different reception once you try it out. This feedback session can help you hone your style for improved delivery.

As much as you may want to reminisce, remember to include statements looking toward the future as the couple begins a new life together. This can be the time to inject inspiring words of encouragement with a toast to the newlyweds. Remember to keep the speech and the toast short and to the point so that the reception stays focused on the bride and groom on their big day.

With plenty of preparation, wedding speeches can be poignant and memorable moments in a day's celebration. Your family and friends, along with the bride and groom, may appreciate the extra thought and effort you put into good delivery. Remember that your words can resonate long after the reception is over as attendees remember your special words dedicated to the newly married couple.

As it is already known that, a best man has numerous duties to perform in a wedding. From keeping the groom organized to meting all his needs and wants on the day of his wedding are some of the duties of a best man. But the most important responsibility that surpasses all, is giving a speech as the groom's best man at the wedding reception party. This is called The Best Man's Speech. There is an appropriate structure for doing it:

1: Breaking the Ice – Do not take this literally, this means starting of your speech by mingling with the bridal party and all the guests. You can do this by making some light comments or with some humor but avoid over doing it though. Since, a best man is a groom's best friend generally; he can make a joke or poke fun at the groom or something. But joking about his bride is a complete no-no and not all would gulp this down in good spirit.

2: Addressing the Bride – The wedding day is the most special day for any bride and groom. But for a bride it is more special, because it is something like a dream comes true. Clichéd as it may sound, it is true! Therefore, you can make it extra special by giving her compliments and how stunning she is looking on this day etc. Maybe you can also compliment her by saying that her groom is very lucky to have found a bride like her.

In this shower of compliments, do not forget to compliment the maid of honor and the entire bridesmaid, as they are the confidantes of the bride. Making them angry means, becoming bad in the eyes of the bride, which you would not want!

3: Self-Introduction – You are no superman that everyone would be awestruck and you do not expect all, present in the room to know you. So, first introduce yourself and let others know how you know the groom, or how long you have known each other. It would be also great to talk about the activities that you both have done together. Talking about activities together does not mean blurting out all his secrets! Tell all about your feeling when you were asked to be the groom's best man and share your emotions in a short and crisp manner.

4: Addressing the Groom – Being the best man is equal to knowing a lot about the groom than anyone present in the room. So, you will not be running out of materials to reflect upon and use them in your speech. You would also remember some embarrassing situations that the groom or both of you had experienced, which is completely funny. So, use these in your speech. This way the attention would be on you while you give your speech. Talk about the growing up years with the groom. In fact, it would be really fun, if props are used, for example, groom's diary or something personalized, which you had. These could be used and talk about, to keep the personal spirits alive on the special day of your friend's.

5: Speak about the newly weds – After all the talks, poking fun at the groom, complimenting the bride and her bridesmaids, it is time to set your tone and talk about your happiness and feeling about your friend finding the girl of his dreams. Let others know how happy you are for the couple and hope that they remain like this forever. Refer to their plans, their future, career, honeymoon etc. You can also share that by this you are not losing but gaining another friend, here the bride! Give them few marriage tips and throw some marriage jokes. All these have to be done in the lightest manner, as much as possible.

6: Close your speech with a toast – Prior to the end of your speech, invite all present at the reception to join you in toasting to the bride and groom. Request them to raise their glasses and celebrate this moment of love and union, by offering toast to the couple in honor of their divine marriage.

Preparations for Your Speech

The tuxedo, the ring and then the speech! You cannot run away from this one if you are the best man. A speech for the reception or even at the rehearsal dinner is required. Keys to a good speech are all in proper planning and practice. You can use some ideas before performing your biggest task as the Best Man.

Consideration towards the ceremony and towards the couple: Match your speech that with the wedding tone. Like say, if the wedding is having casual and a midday affair type, then the speech should be appropriately lighthearted and humorous. If the wedding is of an affair of black or white tie, having a long list of guests, then the speech has to be kept subtle and formal. In this case, sharing some college moments, pranks, etc. of your friend would be a complete bad idea, and certainly not the best of all options.

Selection of an opening: Toastmaster International, which is a reputed organization of speech making, recommends that the speech's start should contain some humorous elements that would draw the attention of all guests present. This can be inclusive of some funny quote or saying, related to marriage or some funny one-liner would do too.

The best option would be to make use of anecdotes that are self-effacing either about your friend or the time when you both met each other.

Limitation of time: If your speech is too short then it is an indication of your lack of interest and thoughts for the groom or that there is an absence of any memorable ones. Try to limit the duration of your speech to 10 minutes maximum. Follow this order:

- Speech opening, with or without funny anecdote
- Story related to the couple
- Good wishes and advice for the couple
- Closing, by inviting all guest to raise a toast for the bride and groom

Deep Breaths: After writing and practicing your speech, take few deep breaths and try to calm yourself and also your nerves prior to the speech deliverance. Using alcohol as a form of alternative to ease yourself and your nervousness is not at all a good idea. This is because the result would end up as bad speech and embarrassment too.

Speech: Etiquette

Any responsibility requires organization and being a best man needs more than that. First, read through sequentially, from the start to the end. This way you can acquire a solid grounding prior to your speech preparation. If there is a presence of sections that consists of information, with what you are already familiar, then move over but do not completely leave it out. Most important thing to know is proper wedding speech along the lines of etiquette.

(a) Learning speech timings, depending whether it is formal, informal or a buffet wedding.
(b) Comprehending the duties of a toastmaster is vital, and if there is an absence of one, then which are the duties that would fall to a best man.

(c) Learning about who says and what or when. It is rather vita to comprehend what you are most expected to say.

(d) Knowledge about the difference that is between a toast and a speech and know about the person you have to raise your toast to.

(e) Learning to deal with various announcements and surprises, to any kind of embarrassment or the cause of offense.

Speech: Preparation

(a) Learning how to plan and make preparations effectively for your speech.

(b) Getting tips and suggestions for researching your speech.

(c) Learning about the duration of your speech, on the dependence of wedding type.

(d) Understanding the nuances and how to structure your speech, inclusive of all the tips and ideas, on getting started.

(e) Learning ways to make a smooth flowing speech because they are written for the purpose of speaking and not to be read out.

Speech: Rehearsing

(a) Learning all the techniques for rehearsing your speech effectively, to let it flow logically and without sounding disjointed.

(b) Learning ways to tell a good story.

(c) Understanding the usage of language that with precision. Ensuring the audience interest and maintenance of it, is a vital matter of importance.

(d) Learning various techniques and ways to keep feelings and emotions intact in your speech.

(e) Discovering comic timing and timing of the funny anecdotes.

Speech: Conquering the nerves

(a) Learning of all techniques that are proven and tested for overcoming anxiety and nerves.
(b) Using tips on the usage of nervous energy for your advantage.
(c) Using tips if really and out-out nervous.

Speech: Charismatic deliverance

(a) Learning ways to deliver a charismatic speech.
(b) Using exercises for vocal improvement and deliverance of good voice throw.
(c) Discovering the development of your presence, so that the audiences are glued to you!
(d) Learning ways to use your hands.
(e) Using tips for achieving good posture.

If there is no time for any preparation or very little, for the matter of fact, then you should take this suggestion and refer to various sample best man speeches and the various templates available in different websites. Do some modifications and add some personal stuff, change some names here and there and voila!

Great Ideas of a Best Man Toast

It is a part of the tradition that a best man does the deliverance of the wedding reception's first toast. His toast has a lot of significance to it. It can offer some really thought proving aspects and view to life of marriage honor the relationship with the groom or even do some revelation of intimate or embarrassing moments in the courtship of the couple. The toast traditionally is a short and simple speech delivered verbally. However, a best man is given complete freedom to try out various approaches connected to the toast. This can be for example, a video presentation or a slideshow. He can also choose in delivering verbal toast, containing some twists and turns.

Traditional: As per the tradition, a best man's speech is completely verbal. This is delivered earlier in the wedding reception. Though this is not original, it is quite a popular and accepted form of toast. If it is a married best man, then he can take the time in offering some advice to enjoy a marital bliss, in pure joy and happiness. He might also simply wish to state why he has so much admiration for the couple and offer all his best wishes and blessings.

There is yet another popular and accepted option to this traditional form of toast making. This is to regale all the guests, with some stories in connection to the groom, either serious or funny that had taken place in the past. If there are mostly conservative and uptight guests then this mode cannot be used because of any occurrence of embarrassment.

Slideshows: This concept of a slideshow is becoming increasingly popular in weddings. Best men are using this concept in offering their speeches and toasts. You can do this and take the advantage of the evening in displaying a slideshow presentation of some pictures of the bride and groom, when they were bachelors and when they became engaged etc. Then there is another option that can be used; this is to take the couple's parents' interviews before the wedding, asking them to give some pictures of their children ranging from the childhood to their adulthood days. You can also ask them some questions, related to the bride and groom's childhood, teens and their adult lives. Then arrange the pictures in the form of a slideshow presentation and narrate all the information in the form of a story or even show the interviews taken of their parents. This is very popular, especially with the elderly generation present in the wedding. This is because they knew the wedded couple as children and now they are all grown ups. So, they become nostalgic by viewing the reminiscence of the old times via the slideshow of stories and pictures.

Songs or Poems: If a best man possesses any linguistic inclination, then he is free to write some short song or a poem in connection with the couple. This little creative piece should be either sentimental or sweet or even funny. In addition, even some that can have a bit of potential embarrassment too. Though he would be making similar points, like that in delivery of a traditional form of speech, the usage of song or poem makes the entire affair a more personal and filled with sentiments. This is more original and quite amusing for all the people present as guests.

Video: Use of videos or a presentation of it is another new and unique method to raise a toast. You can do this, by arranging meetings inclusive of friends, family and loved ones of the couple. Ask them various interesting questions, related to love, relationships, etc. and record them as a video. This is the best idea for a best man, who gets jitters in making speeches or who has a tendency to forget things to say at a wedding. This video concept would allow him to rehearse his speech, repeatedly with the recording of the video, until it has achieved perfection to the core.

Memory boxes: Memory boxes are yet another original toast making ideas. As a best man, you can have a chat with the couple's parents prior to the day. Get all the pasts, in the form of pictures, gifts, favorites, blankets, toys etc. Then after acquiring all, place each of the stuff in one box and let the other remain empty. When the speech or toast making time arrives, you can present each boxes to the couple, which they have to open and tell any story related to it. Then the second empty box would be given, so that they can fill it up with memories that they would make together henceforth.

Things to Do and Not to Do

Best Man toasts actually means speeches. While making the toast to the bride and groom, raising a glass and thinking of saying few words simply, wishing marital bliss to the newly married, in fact you need to do a lot of preparation for this particular day and act. It is not only a day of duty and responsibility for the couple but as a best man, also for you, in fact more. If it so happens that you are not able to write a toast, then it is best to ask someone to assist you in it or better search various websites and get few lines from sample speeches and toasts.

When the time arrives for making the toast actually, then keep in mind to choose the topic that you want to talk.

Moreover, remember that the topic is suitable for everyone present in the reception. You can choose to be funny, hilarious or plain simple but prevent yourself being rude and corny. This is because not only you and the groom's friends are present but also his parents, elders and his newly wedded wife too.

You might crack a joke or two when in the company of your friends and buddies but dare not to crack it all in a speech and amongst wedding guests. You might think that a particular story regarding the groom is down right hilarious but check whether it will go down well with the guests too. If not, then please avoid it. Deciphering aspects and situations is very important. Therefore, it is advisable to use discretion and utmost!

Follow this very vital rule: Drink less or even do not drink at all, so that you are able to stand up and deliver your speech. There have been wedding receptions, where the best men could barely stand straight leave alone give their speeches. This happens to become a part of gossips, embarrassing moments and ill wedding situations. There are some best men who become naturally funny, when they gulp a drink or two that is. But the problem lies in the fact that most of them are not.

A drunken best man and his toasts offend more than entertain. And when a person is drunk, he tends to blurt out things that he is not meant to. So, there are high chances that in a drunken state, he would blurt out incidents, stories etc. that he is not suppose to say, since he at this state loses all power of determination and sensibility.

The toasts are entertaining until they are stuck within the various laid out boundaries. This is in relation to behavior and topics that are appropriate. Additionally to the stories and funny incidents, jokes, etc. about the bride and groom, poking fun at the institution of marriage and talking about the various differences between a man and a woman, within funny connotation are quite popular.

One thing to keep in mind is that re-invention of wheel is not required. Toast offered by a best man in a wedding reception is the most awaited one because people are always in need of some entertainment and they know that they would surely get it from the best man. Do all your homework with utmost hard work and conviction. Remember one thing, the groom has chosen you because he thinks that you are worthy of the job as a best man. Therefore, you do not want to offend or break his trust. Give your best 'Best Man' speech and toast!

Elements to Consider before Writing the Speech

The speech of the best man should be successful and respectful, but also funny. Hence, there is a need for you to note some comments about the bride and groom from your experiences. These are comments that should be personal and sincere, and you should ensure your words are suitable for a general audience of all ages. These require you to create a fine line between irreverence and respect.

There is a need of making personal observations but also ensure they are understood and appreciated by an audience. When you plan to write your best man speech, you should consider the personality of the groom. For example, the groom could be a prankster who laughs easily. He could be someone who really appreciates a good joke at his own expense. In such cases, the speech should reflect the groom's personality and you should make attempts of including funny comments.

At times you can also try to go a bit ahead of funny jokes, but not loose your balance or say something in appropriate. There some grooms who tend to be more traditional, serious or over-romantic. In such cases, you should reflect these personality traits and you should try to make these speeches more complementary and respectful anecdotes. Some jokes are the perfect way for creating the balance them with plenty of sincere and respectful comments.

One of the most commonly forgotten factors while making the speech is the length of the speech. Remember that you should not make the speech very lengthy, as a long speech is not something the one expects from a best man. Your speech should include some quick jokes about the bride and the groom, or even their bridesmaids. However, you should not go overtly long with your speech and the general rule is that shorter is usually better. Usually a speech of about 2-4 minutes is perfect for the best man, and gets him maximum attention.

Now that you have most of these details ready for the speech, you should also make sure that you include a series of incidents from the groom and your life.

Posture and Etiquettes for the Best Man

Being funny is the most vital factor for the best man but there are many other aspects that one should consider here. For example, you should always stand up to speak or say the speech. When you are making the speech, your hands should be raised with the glass of champagne. As you start the speech, make sure that others are seated and quiet. To ensure this you can tap the glass with a spoon to get everybody's attention.

You should appear relaxed while making the speech and no traces of nervousness should be there. You should stand up when the time is right and usually the best man is called upon to deliver the speech. One of the other extremely important factors here is that you do not drink too much before the speech. As a best man, you are also given many other responsibilities apart from giving the speech.

Hence, you need delay your own fun of drinking until you have fulfilled your responsibility towards the groom and bride. As a best man, there can be no greater breach of etiquette and so drinking heavily should be strictly avoided. Else, you would be giving a speech that is slurred or incomprehensible.

You are the best man and everybody expects something really funny from you. Keep in mind that a powerful speech cannot come devoid of supportive body language.

With optimistic body language, you can be guaranteed that all eyes are focused on you. If you want attention from the guests then you have to behave in a similar way. Inappropriate body language while making a speech leads to loss of attention.

Here are a few tips that can help you to reflect positive body language

- Maintaining an upright body posture
- Keeping the hands raised while making the toast
- Smiling or laughing while talking
- Show emotions on the face including smirks
- Keep constant eye contact with the couple and the guests

Being chosen as the best man is actually an honor in itself and hence you should make sure that you justice to this honor. As you are making the speech there should be both excitement and emotions in your speech. Facial expressions should compliment the lines that are reading or saying. Try to modulate your voice according to the theme of the speech.

For instance, being loud while cracking jokes is absolutely all right, but saying something humorous with non-committal expressions would confuse the guests. Hence, you should try to talk and act in a way that impresses the guest, and creates the apt mood for the speech.

Another problem that a lot of best man's go through during the speech is that they get nervous and start perspiring and fumbling. However, these factors reflect poor body language and so there is a need for you to appear confident even if your knees are getting weak. Also, avoid wiping sweat constantly and if you think that you perspire a lot then choose a position near an air-conditioner or fan.

Best Man Basic Speech Format

The basic format for all speeches includes the opening lines, the use of some jokes and quotes, and finally concluding with wedding wishes.

The opening remarks of the best mans speech-

The opening remarks of the best man speech helps to determine if the speech is going to be something funny or boring. There is no doubt that one of the most difficult aspects of giving the best man speech is the opening line. It should be kept in mind that the first sentence or two would be setting the tone for the whole speech. One significant tip here is avoiding the enticement of commencing with a big joke or outrageous comment.

Nevertheless, you should remember that it is much better to start simply and respectfully. It is best to save these jokes for later and more personal comments in the speech. One of the tried and tested methods of delivering the best man's speech is to begin simple and respectfully.

You should then move on to humorous observations and jokes as the speech continues. The need is to start with basic introductions and the relation that you share with the groom and then wrap things up on a sentimental and congratulatory tone. Basically, one can call this a sandwich technique since you are starting with polite and sincere comments, using funny stories and jokes in the middle and then ending off on the congratulatory and emotional note.

Sample

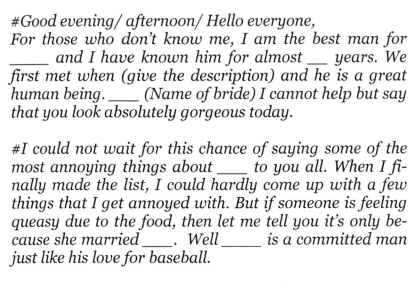

#Good evening/ afternoon/ Hello everyone,
For those who don't know me, I am the best man for
_____ and I have known him for almost ___ years. We
first met when (give the description) and he is a great
human being. ____ (Name of bride) I cannot help but say
that you look absolutely gorgeous today.

#I could not wait for this chance of saying some of the
most annoying things about ____ to you all. When I fi-
nally made the list, I could hardly come up with a few
things that I get annoyed with. But if someone is feeling
queasy due to the food, then let me tell you it's only be-
cause she married ____. Well _____ is a committed man
just like his love for baseball.

#Let me just say that the influential years that I spent in
the company of the groom has contributed largely in de-
veloping my sense of humor. Even though I have tried to
make this speech as funny as possible, please blame him
if you think this is not funny.

 # Ladies and Gentlemen all the bridesmaids look abso-
lutely smashing today, but they are outshone by our
bride, _____. This is a sad day for all of us because
another beauty leaves the 'available list'.

There is some other that you can work on to write a best
man speech. As you write the best man, you should try
and adapt to make a nice decent best man's speech. Some
other ways of spicing the speech include funny best man
speech jokes, which are also easily available.

One factor that should be adhered to here is that if you want to deliver a real stunner then you have to be well organized with all the resources ready much before the wedding day.

There is one more thing that you should remember when you are ending your speech. This includes thanking those who invited you to speak and congratulating the couple. It should be kept in mind that you should always congratulate the bride and the groom before ending your speech. There is a need for you to thank them and the other guests.

If you are close to the groom's family then you should also try to thank them for the honor. Using too many names in the speech is not suggested because you should always try to keep the speech short.

Personalize Your Speech

It is not possible for everybody to be creative enough to write his or her own speeches. Hence, many of the best men try to choose speeches from e-books like this to get some references about speeches. It has been seen that personalizing the speech in your own way is the best method of using them.

Remember that there are many other people using these speeches and hence it may happen that your guests might have heard of the speech before. Therefore, you should try to personalize the speech as much as possible, and cite your incidents rather than taking exactly what is being provided to you.

For example, you can try to adopt some incidents of your own in the speech rather than using the ones listed in the samples. These samples are there to provide you with a comprehensive speech background, but you can make it more interesting by adding your personal touch.

If you are using a ready-made speech then it is best to try to make it short. The short speeches are considered some of the best because the audience does not like long boring wedding speeches. Hence, you should make it a point to keep the wedding speech short and funny. There are certain situations that you have to adapt yourself too with the sample speeches. For example, if you are using the speech of friend, but are the groom's brother, then you should change the sentences as per your requirement.

It is not mandatory to use these speeches as it is and you have the liberty to alter them as per your convenience. If you were the groom's brother then you would find it rather easier to make a speech about the same family.

You should also try to make the speech more personalized, as this is the golden rule of public speaking. Remember that the guests have the ability to say if you are being natural or not. Most people understand that public speaking can make you nervous and they would be sympathetic. So do not get nervous about a couple of errors here and there. Try to keep yourself composed and make sure that you do not make any more mistakes.

Try to be comfortably focused on the more important matters that have to be done later like attending to the other dignitaries and participants. You should remember that your speech is one of the fun parts of the day, and thus there is no need for you to panic.

Try to opt for speeches and instances that come spontaneously rather than by copying the styles of others. Keep a note of all the things that you want to say about the groom and then formulate it in your own words. This would make you more confident and cause less embarrassment because you are not saying anything that has been copied.

Since you have now taken a decision to give the best man's speech, you can also refer to the internet, for videos so that can get a better idea of making the speech. Instead of only preparing for your own speech, you should also consult with others. There is a great deal of anxiety that you are dealing with and there is also a lot of work that has to be done now and similar to any other speeches prepared earlier, you should rehearse it well, like the common saying that practice makes a man perfect and you can turn out to be the perfect and elegant guy, if you know your subject thoroughly and are comfortable with what you are saying.

Watch Out of the 'Slip of Tongue'

The best man is always considered one of the most important characters in the wedding. The speech that he is expected to give is also supposed to be something filled with humor and a faint touch of emotions. The best man speeches are usually expected to be filled with jokes and quotes but not wild humor. Remember that often these wedding speeches are one of the main reasons for the couple ending up in a fight immediately after the ceremony.

Hence, you should make sure that you are not standing there and spilling out secrets that should have been left unsaid. In addition, certainly there should be no mention of the stripper at the bachelor party. Humor is the key essence of your speech but if used in the wrong way this can totally spoil your speech. Hence, you should try to use humor in the right way and crack jokes, which keeps the audiences entertained rather than leaving them appalled.

Many relationships are spoiled after the wedding speeches because the drunken best man talks only about ex-girlfriends and past affairs in the speech and completely forgets about the wedding. There are some revelations in the speeches that should not have been discussed. A lot of people who get drunk and say things in their toasts, and this can actually lead to spoiling relationships forever. This is one of the main reasons that it is suggested that you keep away from getting drunk before the speech.

Some common mistakes that the best man should always avoid include-

Giving drunken speeches- If you are still not over from the hangover of the previous night then it is best to let someone else do the speech, or better to just say that there is no speech. Drunken best man's can spoil the show for the bride and the groom, and this is not how you would want to be remembered. So avoid getting drunk during the wedding or before the wedding too.

Getting loads of notes- No doubt that you are the best man and have thought of scores of jokes to be cracked at the wedding. However, it should be remembered that seeing the notes would make half the guests fall asleep. This usually results in guest getting up to get their plates full or falling asleep. Getting too many notes would also mean that you never know what you want to say and get confused. Thus, it is suggested that you should focus on improvisation before preparing the final draft. Get a copy of the speech that is free from scratches and crosses.

Not rehearsing your speech. Now you would not want to make your toast while digging your eyes into the paper. It is best to rehearse your speech in advance so that you can look up in to the eyes of the guests and the bride and the groom. Making eye contact is also very essential, as you would not want to be reading out of the paper all the time and expect the guests to keep laughing at your jokes. To make things humorous even your expressions and body language should be funny.

Getting too clandestine or open. Since most guests know that you are the best man, they assume that you would also know many details about the bride and the groom. However, mentioning code words or trying to wink constantly while looking at the groom would make everyone else uncomfortable. No doubt that you have a lot to share here, but since it is very obvious that you cannot it is best to avoid bringing up very secretive topics or those incidents that are very personal to share.

Using depressing speech topics. As the best man, you are expected to get up there and cheer up the guests and communicate best wishes. Even if humor is not something that you are very good at, you can try to retain a smile on your face. If you cannot crack too many funny jokes then just stick to relating a few incidents from the past of the bride and the groom.

It is best to stick to the groom, but you can also talk about the bride if you know her well. For example, if the groom had a pet that he loved tremendously then you should mention it in the toast by saying
'Here's a toast from me and (Name of pet) or say that if it had been there then he or she would be cheering for you too. Do not make the speech too depressing and take away the day from them.

Using sex in the speech. You would certainly not want to crack a sex joke here unless you are trying to be really immodest. Weddings are a special occasion and no matter how much you thought that the bachelor party was wild, sex is a topic that should not be a part of your speech. Weddings are not the best occasion for cracking such jokes and you should save them for parties and gatherings.

Not reading the draft. You must practice your speech before making the toast, because with a little practice you can make the speech more spontaneous. Those who do not read their speeches prior to making the toast end up looking at notes rather than looking at guests. You should try to read your drafts to ensure that there are no errors in it. Often, the best man ends up giving their speeches with the wrong draft, or say things, which makes no sense. Thus, your focus should be to make the speech aloud in front of someone else and ask him or her to comment on it.

Not wishing the couple.Therefore, you are the best man who is all set to crack jokes about wedding and the groom. But in the entire event, it can happen that you would forget to wish the bride and the groom. It has happened a lot of times when the best man has cracked his joke, done his jester act and forgotten to wish the couple on their wedding. Ultimately, you are speaking in the wedding and if you fail to congratulate the couple then the complete attempt of making the speech is useless. You should also thank the groom for providing you the opportunity of making a speech in their honor.

Some things that are best left unsaid at weddings include-

- Ex-girlfriends and flings
- Using negative attitude towards the wedding, or the couple
- Too many clichés that would put the guests to sleep
- Not being in harmony with the wedding theme
- Being snobbish or overtly scholarly
- Cracking jokes that would embarrass anyone
- Mentioning too many awkward phrases or comments
- Using anecdotes that are unsuitable for the situation
- Mentioning earlier marriages or divorces
- Getting drunk
- Be gloomy or negative in your speech
- Forget to pass on good wishes to the bride and the groom

As you are making a speech you should always focus on fondness towards the groom while using a bit of fun element. Remember that clichés cannot be used through out the toast and there is a need for you to add some personal jokes to the speech to prevent it from getting. Try to avoid clichés and try to re-create them in your own innovative way. Certain wedding ceremonies can be pretty formal, and in such gatherings, using scholarly texts are appropriate. However, you are the best man and if someone has the right to crack some whacky jokes, it is you.

It should be kept in mind that no matter how much you want to talk about the number of girls that your best friend has slept with, you should not mention anything that is embarrassing or humiliates him. When you are composing a toast, avoid stating anything that is awkward. You can crack some honeymoon jokes or mention casual facts, but stay away from talking about intimate moments of the couple. Use phrases that are appropriate for others present there, and make every one smile.

Your friend circle is present there in a smaller number, and if you want to get really wild, then the bachelor party is the right time. The others who are present in small numbers would restrict your applause. Try adding humor to the toast in a subtle and appealing way. The toast should always finish on a somber note of wishing the bride and the groom all the best, after all that is why you are making the speech.

This may not be your first best man speech for your best friend but you should make sure any reference to their previous marriages or affairs should be avoided. You should simply take no notice of knowing any such detail and keep your speech focused on the couple. Some of the few things that you should forget here include wild incidents that embarrass others and this could be related to their personal history.

Facts You Can't Go Without

There are a lot of interesting facts about the best man's speech that you should remember while making your speech and saying it. These are factors that would help you to appear more confident and help you to write things in a natural and spontaneous way.

Fact 1#

The speech of the best man speech is one of the lighter speeches through out the wedding. Therefore, it is really all right for you to use a lot of humor and wit. One of the major factors that make the speech funny is that they are in a way, held by a man, and for a man. Since no man is really comfortable talking about their feelings, they try to cover it up with humor.

Fact 2#

This speech reflects upon the groom and is a reflection of someone who cares a great deal about him. The convey-ing of feelings should be of support and letting the groom know that he is best suited for the bride, and you are there to stand by his side at the altar to support him. Many people expect jokes about the groom in his speech and this is why a funny story is told in the speech.

Fact 3#

The focuses of these speeches are always on the groom and hence you should try to combine fun with some good qualities of the groom. Apart from cracking jokes, these speeches should also try to bring out the positive qualities of the groom as a new husband.

Fact 4#

Jokes and quotes can be combined to create a fun element in the wedding. The use of quotes and jokes together in contrast is one of the best means of cracking jokes. This is a fun way of trying to communicate your best wishes to the groom and expressing some of the best moments of your life.

A Formal Speech Example

Good evening/ afternoon to everyone,
I have been given the honor of being the best man to
_____, and I cannot thank him enough for it. There are a
few thank-yous that I would like to make here. First, it
goes to those who have helped in the service, and made
this such a lovely party. These thanks are for all those
who have contributed to the wedding by helping in deco-
ration, getting food or even just to support the happy
couple.

The second thanks are to all the lovely bridesmaids who
have done a magnificent job in helping the bride today.
All of you look amazing, and here is a big thanks to you
too. Finally, I want to thank the beautiful bride for turn-
ing up today because _____ was worrying, and it
wasn't a pretty sight. On his behalf, he has asked me to
tell you that he could not have made a better choice, and
he would get into in more detail in his speech.

Now, I have known ____ for _____amount of years now.
It is not easy to know someone this well the way that I
know all his little habits. And I can't express how annoy-
ing he can become after a few pints. And this is just a
little warning to you all there! However, he has always
helped me through some hard times, and over these
years, he has been there to support me. And I know he
will also support his new bride the same way.

I was given the task to keep ____ clean for the wedding and not embarrass him too much. And I do want to say that he is one of the few people who are always up for a laugh, and lives life to the max.

I remember when we were-(here you should narrate some funny incident of the past).

Before _____ met _____, he found it hard to talk to women and was honestly sucked at it. But he would still get some of the most gorgeous women, but no one could match up to our lovely bride here. I have seen how _____ changed his life for the better and how happier and energetic he has been since then.

I had been once told me that Love can effortlessly be affected by physical appearance. (Name of the bride), I am sure that when you saw_____ there were no confusions. ____ had told me once that he didn't believe in love at first sight. But after meeting (name of bride) all that has changed.

Finally, I would like thank everybody for coming and joining the newly married couple in their celebrations. We all agree they make a fantastic couple and so ladies and gentlemen, please join me in a toast.

Here is to the happy couple, may their love last forever! Cheers!

Wedding Jokes and Quotes

Here are some popular jokes and quotes that you can use in the best man speeches.

Good Wedding Jokes

I can sincerely say that in all the years of friendship, I have never heard anyone question _____ intelligence. Honestly, I never heard anyone even talk about any intelligence on ____ part.

_____it'sall right muttering some words in the church and discover that you are married, but if you mumble a few words in your sleep, there are chances that you would be thrown out of the house.

Ladies and Gentlemen, if anyone here is feeling, worried, nervous or uneasy it is probably because she just got married to _____.

I've know ____ for quite some time now and am considered a bit of a father figure since I witnessed him crawl around on his knees. And drink from a bottle and also helped him to clean up after the Bachelor Party.

A lady once said that I my husband a millionaire. Her impressed friend asked what he was before he married her. And she replied, "A multi-millionaire".

They say that speech making is a similar to prospecting for black gold. If you do not strike oil in a few minutes, you should stop boring.

I am told that some of the best speechmakers follow three simple rules like standing up. Speaking and very quickly, shutting up too and I will try to stick to that advice.

The brain is a magnificent thing, as it never stops functioning since you're born until the moment you stand up to make a speech. - Herbert V Prochnow and Herbert V Prochnow Jnr

You can't blame everything on the government! That is why you need a wife - Unknown

"How to be Happy Though Married" - book by Rev. E.J.Hardy, 1910

The only advice to a person who is about to marry is- Don't. - Unknown

Let's have a wedding - Charles Dickens (Great Expectations)

Marriage has many pains, but celibacy has no pleasure - Dr. Johnson

Composed that monstrous animal a husband and a wife - Henry Fielding

The bridal day, which is not long... - Spenser

The guest are met, the feast is set
May'st hear the merry din
- Samuel Taylor Coleridge

Wedlock, indeed, hath oft compared been
To public feasts, where meet a public rout
Where they that are without would fain go in
And they that are within would fain go out
- Sir John Davies (17c.)

I think men with a pierced ear are better prepared for marriage since they have already experienced pain and bought jewelry. (Rita Rudner)

Keep your eyes wide open before the wedding, half shut afterwards. (Benjamin Franklin)

By all means marry; if you get a good wife, you'll be happy. If you get a bad one, you'll become a philosopher. (Socrates)

A husband is like a house on fire if he goes out when unattended. (Evan Esar)

My wife dresses to kill and sadly she cooks the same way. (Henny Youngman)

My wife and I were happy for thirty years and then we met. (Rodney Dangerfield)

A good wife always forgives her husband when she's wrong. (Milton Berle)

I love being married because you fine one special person to annoy for the rest of your life. (Rita Rudner)

Never go to bed mad. Stay up and fight. (Phyllis Diller)

All marriages are mixed marriages. (Chantal Saperstein)

There's only one way to have a happy marriage. When I learn it I'll get married again. (Clint Eastwood)

The secret of a happy marriage remains a secret. (Henny Youngman)

The most excellent way to get husbands into listening to you is suggesting that they're too old to do it. (Ann Bancroft)

Wedlock or deadlock? That is the question!

Why such a big deal? What excitement what commotion and fuss-over a single hour of one day in our life!

Is marriage much ado about nothing- or something much to do about everything?

Why do people still get married as they have since times immemorial? Why, if half later get divorced?

Where did marriage come from – and where is it going?

Wedding Quotes

Using wedding quotes or one-liner's is a popular way of lightening the atmosphere and bringing in a little humor into the wedding. Quotes like speeches can be funny or sincere.

They can either have you in splits or make your thought process screech to a halt and sit up and think twice! Whichever ones are used they often have a positive effect and help in bringing the speech to a grand finale.

Quotes by Famous People

Elvis Presley, 1935 - 1977, Love Me Tender [1956]

Love me tender, love me sweet, never let me go.

Mahatma Gandhi

Where there is love there is life

St. Augustine

Better to have loved and lost, than to have never loved at all.

Samuel Taylor Coleridge

Sympathy constitutes friendship; but in love, there is a sort of antipathy, or opposing passion. Each strives to be the other, and both together make up one whole.

Thoreau

There is no remedy for love but to love more

Alicia Barnhart

True love never dies, for it is lust that fades away. Love bonds for a lifetime but lust just pushes away.

Benjamin Franklin

He that falls in love with himself will have no rivals

Don Byas

You call it madness, but I call it love.

Buddha

He who loves 50 people has 50 woes; he who loves no one has no woes.

Ingrid Bergman

A kiss is a lovely trick designed by nature to stop speech when words become superfluous.

Dr. Martin Luther King, Jr.

He who is devoid of the power to forgive is devoid of the power to love.

Victor Hugo

The supreme happiness in life is the conviction that we are loved.

Mother Theresa

It is easy to love people far away. It is not always easy to love those close to us. It is easier to give a cup of rice to relieve hunger than to relieve the loneliness and pain of someone unloved in our own home. Bring love into your home for this is where our love for each other must start.

If you judge people, you have no time to love them.

Anonymous quotes on love

If you love someone, let them go. If they return to you, it was meant to be. If they don't, their love was never yours to begin with...

Love is hard work; and hard work sometimes hurts!

Who says love never lives? Maybe we've never lived.

Some love lasts a lifetime. True love lasts forever.

If love is great, and there are no greater things, then what I feel for you must be the greatest.

Love is like playing the piano. First, you must learn to play by the rules, and then you must forget the rules and play from your heart.

Quotes from Literature about Love

Ovine [Publius Ovidius Naso],43 B.C. - A.D. C 18 Ibid. II, 107

"To be loved, be lovable."

Love

Love is a friendship that has caught fire. It is quiet understanding, mutual confidence, sharing and forgiving. It is loyalty through good and bad. It settles for less than perfection, and makes allowances for human weakness. Love is content with the present. It hopes for the future and it doesn't brood over the past. It's the day-in and day-out chronicle of irritations, problems, compromises, small disappointments, big victories, and working toward common goals. If you have love in your life, it can make up for a great many things you lack. If you don't have it, no matter what else there is, it is not enough, so search for it, ask God for it, and share it!

Author Unknown

Sooner or later we begin to understand that love is more than verses on valentines and romance in the movies. We begin to know that love is here and now, real and true, the most important thing in our lives. For love, is the creator of our favorite memories, and the foundation of our fondest dreams. Love is a promise that is always kept, a fortune that can never be spent, a seed that can flourish in even the most unlikely of places. And this radiance that never fades, this mysterious and magical joy, is the greatest treasure of all - one known only by those who love.

Sir Hugh Walpole, 1884-1941

The most wonderful of all things in life is the discovery of another human being with whom one's relationship has a growing depth, beauty and joy as the years increase. This inner progressiveness of love between two human beings is a most marvelous thing; it cannot be found by looking for it or by passionately wishing for it. It is a sort of divine accident, and the most wonderful of all things in life.

William Shakespeare,1564 - 1616

Love comforted like sunshine after rain. *l. 799*

Doubt thou the stars are fire; doubt that the sun doth move; doubt truth to be a liar; but never doubt I love you. II, ii, 115

I love thee, I love but thee with a love that shall not die. Till the sun grows cold and the stars grow old.

William M. Thackeray

To love and win is the best thing. To love and lose, the next best.

D.H. Lawrence

Those that go searching for love only make manifest their own lovelessness, and the loveless never find love, only the loving find love, and they never have to seek it.

Louisa May Alcott

Love is a great beautifier.

Best Man's Different Roles

The best man's speech is considered to be one of the funniest and most entertaining speeches in a wedding. Hence, it is true that the best man might have to incorporate some funny incidents in the speech to ensure that the audience is entertained. However, the best man is not always the groom's best friend. Some of the common people who can be the best man at a wedding include-

- Best friend of the groom
- Brother of the groom
- Son of the groom
- Cousin of the groom
- Cousin/ brother of the bride

In all of these cases the best man has to make sure that, the speech made compliments his relationship with the groom and does not lead to any kind of embarrassing confrontation for any of the parties present there.

Best friend of the groom. If you are the groom's best friend then you have to write a best man's speech picturing a close friend with his partner. Here you would have to keep all those people in mind who are important to him and then create the speech. For instance, try to include some details of the history of the couple like how long have they been together or how long have they known each other.

There are some other points that you can add here about the background of his wife to be. Even though this speech is not about her it is vital for you to dedicate at least a paragraph for her. Here you can mention details on what she is like and how she makes your friend feel. Apart from this, you can also mentioned things about what the couple wants from life and their relationship. You have the right to crack the most jokes and keep the groom and guests entertained.

Brother of the groom. As the brother of the groom you can start by saying that, you are like two peas in a pod, or we are as close as close could be or tight knit. However, also include funny punches like- but there are times when I could have easily traded him off with a stranger or would be glad to knock him down. Do say that you love your brother a lot and you have been together through thick and thin.

You can say 'I can't say how happy I am to see that you have found the perfect woman for you. This is one of the biggest steps that you took towards your future, and gave me a wonderful sister in law. Many congratulations to my playmate, my confidant, my brother and my one of my dearest friends.'

You can mention a few things about your family traditions and crack jokes. Those who are not very close to their brothers can make the speech formal with some funny childhood incidents.

Son of the groom- This can be an awkward stage to give the speech but you should make sure that you convey your best feelings to your dad and the new bride to be. If your parents are divorced and ended things on a good term, or if your mother is no more then you can wish them on her behalf. However, in cases where the relation is strained it is best not to mention any such things. Instead, you should just stick to a simple and funny speech without any references to their second marriages.

Cousin of the groom. The cousin of the groom can be a close friend or he can also be someone who has met the groom recently. Long distance cousins are often chosen for the role of the best man. In such cases, you should try to find out some details about the bride and the groom and then use it in the speech. As a cousin, you have the freedom for cracking jokes regarding family traditions and other members but your speech should not deviate from the main area.

Brother or cousin of the bride. Often the groom chooses the brother of the bride or the cousin of the bride to be the best man and there are various factors attributing to it. The brother or the cousin may be close to the bride or they can also be just related because of the bride. In such cases, you should try to keep the speech lightly humorous with focus on both your sister and the groom. Funny jokes about weddings in general can be cracked and you should include some family traditions in the speech. Try to find out more about the groom and say that even though you have just known him for while you do not feel that the groom is not a close friend.

Structural Steps to Write a Hilarious and Heartfelt Speech

All best men want to write their speech from the heart but are not very good with creativity. In such cases it is best to choose some samples listed and above and add a few personal incidents to make the speech humorous. A few factors should be followed in sequence order to ensure that you give the perfect speech. These steps should be implemented in the order given-

Collect matter for the speech. These could be incidents, funny stories or habits of the grooms, along with other ideas.

Write your speech at least a week before the wedding- Completing the speech before time ensures that you would have plenty of time to take part in the wedding activities.

Rehearse the speech. This would ensure that you are able to make the speech an interactive session rather than just reading it out.

Make a final copy. A final copy of the speech with key words and notes should be kept for use. Do not take the scribbled and scratched out copy while making the toast.

Introduce yourself. All guests may know that you are the best man, but might not know your name.

Thank the groom- Always thank the groom for his speech, and the person who gave the speech before you.

Finally thank all for attending, including the grooms and the bride's family and parents.

Congratulate the bride and the groom- Wish the bride and groom as a couple and talk about what they are like together, etc.

Include humor- Humor can be added as required through funny stories and incidents, along with jokes and quotes.

Talk about the couple- Talk about the couple as individual persons and make sure that you say a few things about the bride too. For instance, what he is like and what the bride is like.

Comments from groom- Often the groom asks the best man to say a few things on behalf of him, for the bride. In such cases, make sure that you convey these feelings correctly because this is something special for the two of them.

Finale- No speech is complete without a grand finale and hence it is vital for you to congratulate the bride and the groom here, and wish them all the best for their future.

End of the Line

The best man's speech can be enjoyed by the guests only if it comes from the heart. As the best man, you should plan and work on speeches in advance as they can go wrong if they are very long or use the inappropriate content. Your speech should be supportive and enthusiastic with lots of humor.

Remember that the speech should be about things that you are going to say from your heart. If you are a comedian then there is you can use lots of humor but if you are a serious person then you can restrict the number of jokes that you use. Most importantly, these jokes should be clean and do not embarrass anyone.

You must remember that the speech should not be copied off the Internet and you have to use some real life ideas to make the speech personal. These are ideas that can be taken from different sources, including this e-book. However, without personalizing them and adding some pun to them, it would not be a perfect speech.

It is very normal that on the wedding day you would be little nervous prior to your speech. However, you should note the key words or key points so that you do not forget the speech. Make sure that your content is apt for the occasion and there is no harm in asking someone else to hear it before the wedding day.

You should ensure that the speech is perfect in every way, and thus keep it simple with some of the funniest memories that you shared with the groom. As the best man, there are honor duties and responsibilities that have to be followed and it is suggested to rehearse and remember your speech in advance.

Try to keep the maid or matron of honor speech short and simple so that audiences are entertained and enjoy your speech. One can include poems, love quotes and marriage quotes in the speech, and this should be focused on making the couple feel special. You should remember that your speech is supposed to cheer up the couple and lighten the mood after the speech of the father and maid of honor.

At the end of the day, it is the best man who would be the center of attention of all the bridesmaids. Try and use comments from other friends, and there are things that you can say on behalf of the others, including comments that you think would make this moment worthwhile.

Printed in Great Britain
by Amazon.co.uk, Ltd.,
Marston Gate.